Our Town

Healthy Living

This is me.

This is my family.

This is our town.

This is the clock

in our town.

Here is the hospital

in our town.

GV Health

Main Entrance →

Emergency Department Entrance ←

After Hours Hospital Entrance
8.00pm to 7.30am only ←

Totally smoke free

7

GOULBURN VALLEY HEALTH

Here is the library.
We read books
at the library.

Young Readers AGES 7-12

Young Readers AGES 7-12

Young Readers

Young Readers

AGES 7-12

North Pole

9

We go to the swimming pool, when it is hot.

This is the playground.
I play with my friends
at the playground.

These are the shops
in our town.

We love our town.